D0722219

SPHYNX

by Ruth Owen

PowerKiDS press.

New York

Published in 2014 by The Rosen Publishing Group, Inc.
29 East 21st Street, New York, NY 10010

Produced for Rosen by Ruby Tuesday Books Ltd
Editor for Ruby Tuesday Books Ltd: Mark J. Sachner
US Editor: Sara Howell
Designer: Emma Randall

Photo Credits:
Cover, 1, 4–5, 6–7, 8–9, 10–11, 12–13, 14–15, 17, 21, 30 © Shutterstock; 16, 18–19 © istockphoto; 23,
24–25 © Wikipedia Creative Commons; 26–27 © Christopher Voelker: www.voelkerstudio.com;
28 © Allstar Picture Library/Alamy; 28–29 © Warner Bros/Everett/Rex Features.

Library of Congress Cataloging-in-Publication Data

Owen, Ruth, 1967–
 Sphynx / by Ruth Owen.
    p. cm. — (Cats are cool)
 Includes index.
 ISBN 978-1-4777-1281-8 (library binding) — ISBN 978-1-4777-1348-8 (pbk.) —
 ISBN 978-1-4777-1351-8 (6-pack)
 1. Sphynx cat—Juvenile literature. I. Title.
 SF449.S68O94 2014
 636.8—dc23

                            2012047582

Manufactured in the United States of America

CPSIA Compliance Information: Batch #: S13PK7 For Further Information contact: Rosen Publishing, New York, New York at 1-800-237-9932

Contents

Bald and Beautiful

If you are asked to imagine a cat, you might think of a small animal with a long tail, big eyes, and coat of soft, silky fur.

There is one **breed** of cat, however, that doesn't exactly fit that description. Sphynx cats are different from other breeds in one important way. These cats do not have a thick coat of fur!

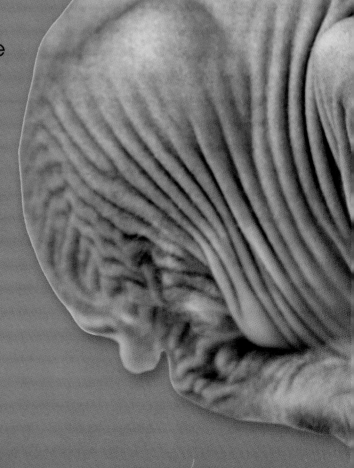

Sphynx cats have caused a lot of arguments among cat lovers. Some cat fans think these animals look like small, ugly space aliens. Sphynx cat owners, however, say their hairless pets are beautiful. One thing everyone agrees on is that these smart, friendly **felines** are one of the most unusual breeds of cat in the world.

A sphynx cat

Perfect Purr Facts

Sphynx cats often look very wrinkled. They actually have no more wrinkles than other cats, though. It's just that their wrinkly skin is always showing!

The First Sphynx Cat

It doesn't happen very often, but occasionally a female cat with a furry coat will give birth to a hairless kitten. This happened in Toronto, Canada, in 1966. A black and white furry cat gave birth to a bald kitten. The kitten's owner named him Prune, after the wrinkled, dried fruit.

Prune's owner decided to develop a breed of hairless cats. When an animal **breeder** wants to create animals that look a certain way, the breeder **mates** males and females that have a similar look. Prune's owner didn't have any other hairless cats, though, so Prune mated with normal, furry females. A small number of Prune's kittens were born bald, but most had fur. So, the plan to create a new breed of wrinkled, hairless cats never got off the ground.

A sphynx cat

Perfect Purr Facts

Prune's bald kittens were known as Canadian hairless cats. Some people started to call them sphynx cats, though, after the ancient Egyptian sphinx. The name stuck! An Egyptian sphinx is a mythical beast with a lion's body and a human head.

An Egyptian sphinx statue

The Sphynx Breed Takes Off

In 1975, a farm cat named Jezabelle gave birth to a hairless kitten in Minnesota. Jezabelle's owners named the kitten Epidermis, which is the word for an outer layer of skin. A year later, Jezabelle had another hairless kitten that was named Dermis.

Epidermis and Dermis were sold to a cat breeder. The breeder mated them with Cornish rex cats, which often have very little fur.

Around the same time, a cat breeder in Ontario, Canada, found three hairless kittens abandoned on a street. Two of these cats, Punkie and Paloma, were bred with a Devon rex cat.

This time, the breeders' plans to breed hairless cats were successful, and the numbers of bald kittens born began to grow. So Epidermis, Dermis, Punkie, and Paloma are the **ancestors** of all the sphynx cats alive today.

A Cornish
rex cat

Perfect Purr Facts

Cornish rex and Devon
rex cats are breeds that
started in the United
Kingdom. These cats often
have very short fur that
grows in curls or waves.
They also have huge ears!

A Devon rex
kitten

The Sphynx Look

Sphynx cats are known as hairless cats, but most of them actually do have a little soft **down**, or fuzz, on their skin. When you stroke a sphynx cat, this fuzzy down makes it feel as if you are stroking a soft, warm peach!

Sphynx cats come in many different colors. Their skin also shows the markings, or pattern, they would have if they had a fur coat. These cats have hard, muscular bodies, and their rounded bellies often look as if they have just eaten a big dinner.

Sphynx cats have large, lemon-shaped eyes that give them a friendly **expression**. They also have huge ears.

10

Perfect Purr Facts

Sphynx cats have thick **pads** on the bottom of their paws. This makes them look a little as if they are walking on cushions.

Pads

A sphynx has skin markings instead of fur markings.

A Monkey, a Dog, a Human, or a Cat?

Some sphynx owners say their superintelligent, loving cats act as if they are part monkey, part dog, part human, and part cat!

Like monkeys, sphynx cats will climb to the highest point in a room just for fun. They love to leap from the top of bookshelves and doors. Like dogs, these cats enjoy playing fetch with their toys. They will also follow their owner from room to room.

Sphynx cats love other cats and even dogs, but they love humans best of all. A sphynx enjoys hanging out with its human family. It will even shoulder surf, or ride around the house on its favorite person's shoulder.

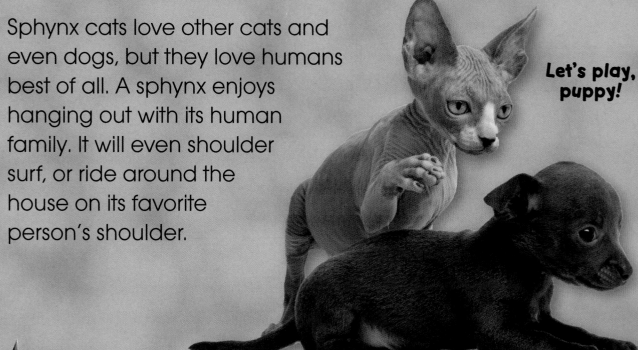

Let's play, puppy!

Perfect Purr Facts

When someone visits its home, a sphynx cat always wants to introduce itself and make a new friend.

What's in here?

What do you mean, this isn't a toy?

Peek-a-boo!

Sphynx Moms

Like all breeds of cat, a female sphynx is old enough to have kittens when she is around six to ten months old.

Cats are pregnant for 60 to 70 days. Most give birth after 66 days.

A pregnant cat's tummy will grow bigger and bigger. She will also feel hungrier than usual and need more food to eat. Toward the end of her pregnancy, she will start to search for a place to be her nest. Usually, a cat will choose a quiet, dark, cozy place such as a closet. When it is time for the kittens to arrive, a female cat will disappear into her nest to give birth.

Perfect Purr Facts

Owners often keep watch to see where their cat moms want to nest. Then they put a cat bed or a cozy cardboard box filled with blankets in her chosen place.

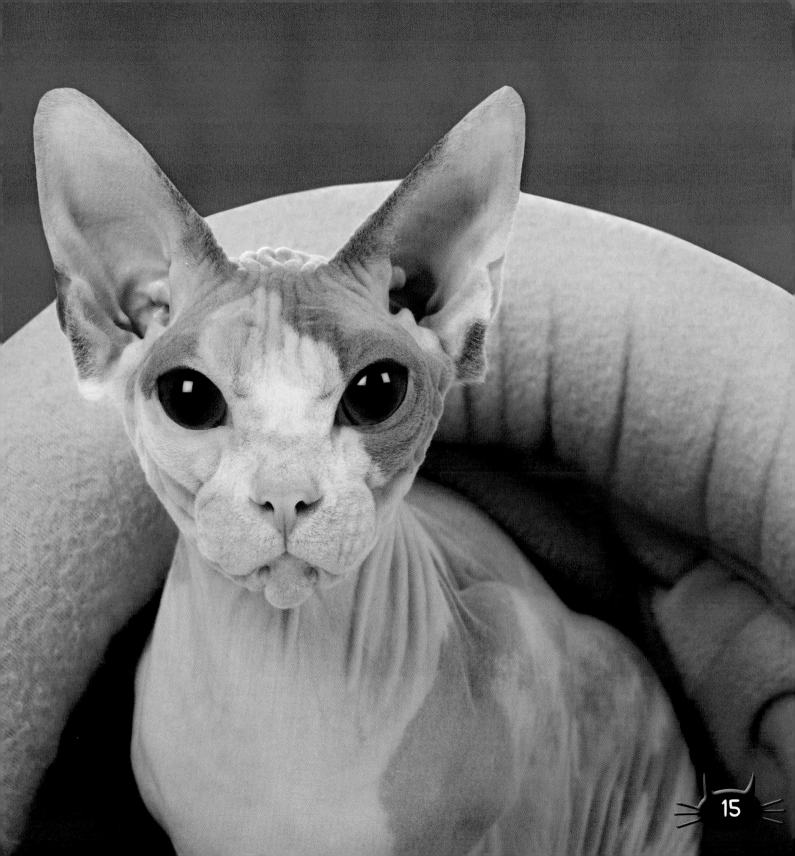

Newborn Kittens

A female cat usually gives birth to a **litter** of between three and six kittens. The newborn kittens cannot see, hear, or walk. They can smell, though, and know their mother by her smell.

Newborn kittens keep warm by snuggling up to their mother's body. They drink milk from her body, too. A mother cat keeps her kittens clean by licking them.

Sphynx kittens' eyes open when they are between five and eight days old. They cannot see properly, however, until they are about five weeks old. At three to four weeks old, the baby sphynx start to walk, but their little legs are very wobbly!

A five-day-old sphynx kitten

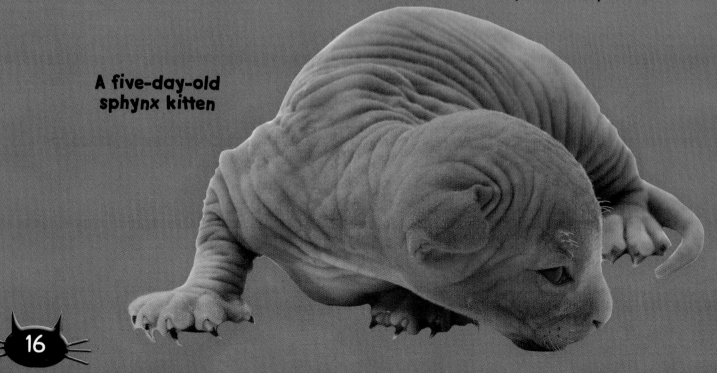

Perfect Purr Facts

When a mother cat leaves the nest to eat or go to the bathroom, the kittens may miss her. They often make tiny, squeaky crying noises to call her back.

A two-week-old sphynx kitten

Kitty Grows Up

Like all kittens, by the time a baby sphynx is four to five weeks old, it will be strong enough to start playing with its brothers and sisters. It may also climb out of the nest to explore its surroundings.

At five weeks old, kittens are able to **groom** themselves by licking their bodies. Their mother will still wash them, too. At this age, kittens can also begin to eat solid food such as canned kitten food. They still drink their mother's milk, though, for several more weeks.

By the time they are eight weeks old, sphynx kittens will be wrestling with their **littermates** or other pets, leaping onto furniture, and even climbing up curtains!

A mother sphynx cat washing its kitten

Perfect Purr Facts

Like adult cats, kittens purr to show they are happy and content. In fact, many kittens will start to purr when they are just two or three days old!

A ten-week-old sphynx kitten

Sphynx Cats as Pets

After about 12 weeks, a sphynx kitten is old enough to leave its mother and go to live with new owners.

Many people have an **allergy** to cats that makes them sneeze or have trouble breathing. Some people think because sphynx cats do not have fur, they are a good pet for a person with an allergy. Sadly, this isn't true. People with allergies are not allergic to cat fur, but to a substance in cats' **saliva**. When a cat licks its body, it covers its fur or skin with this substance. So sphynx cats can still make allergic people unwell.

Perfect Purr Facts

A sphynx cat needs company and should not be left alone all day in an empty house or apartment. If a sphynx's human owners cannot stay home with their pet, they should get their sphynx another cat to hang out with.

Bathtime for Kitty

Sphynx cats lick their bodies to stay clean, but they also need a little extra grooming help from their owners.

Cats' skin produces oil that is soaked up by their fur. The oil keeps the fur in good condition. Sphynx cats do not have fur, but their skin still produces oil. The oil can build up on the cat's skin, becoming greasy and grimy. Once a week, sphynx cat owners must give their pets a soapy bath with a special cat shampoo.

Like most cats, sphynx cats don't always like water. An owner must begin bathing a sphynx kitten when it is young so it gets used to its weekly bath.

Perfect Purr Facts

Unlike furry cats, sphynx cats do not have hairs in their ears to stop dirt and skin oils from getting inside. A sphynx cat's owner must use cotton balls to gently clean the cat's ears.

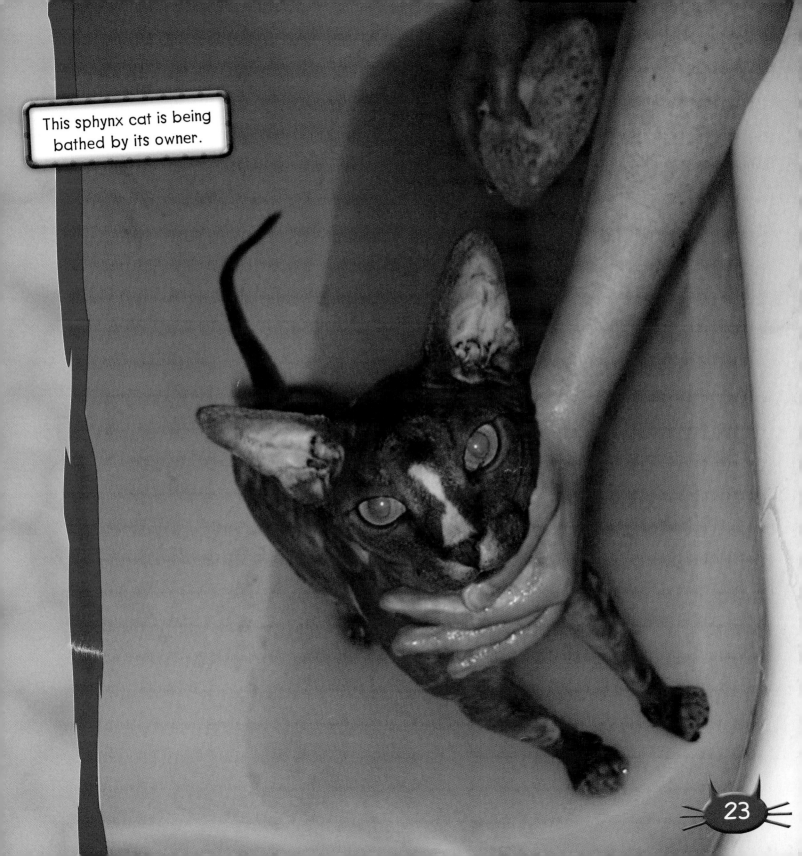

This sphynx cat is being bathed by its owner.

Sphynx Staying Warm

If you were to spend an icy or snowy winter night outside with no clothes on, you might die from the cold. It's the same for sphynx cats!

Unlike their fur-covered cat cousins, sphynx cannot spend time outside when the weather is cold. These hairless cats can even feel cold when they're indoors, so their owners usually keep the heat turned up.

Smart sphynx are very good at searching out heat, though. They doze in sunny windows and snooze on top of warm televisions or computers. They will snuggle under the quilt with their owners and may even cuddle up to a dog for warmth.

Perfect Purr Facts

A sphynx cat should not go outside in the hot sun because its skin can get sunburned.

This sphynx is taking a nap on a sunny sofa.

The Coolest Cats Around

Some sphynx cat owners have found the perfect way to keep their chilly kitties warm with cat clothes!

Sphynx cat owner Melanie Manson had tried using tiny dog clothes and making cat outfits from the arms of sweaters. The clothes just weren't right, however, for her cats' **unique** body shapes and energetic leaping and playing.

So, Melanie turned fashion designer and has created a range of soft, stretchy outfits perfectly designed to fit cat bodies. Now sphynx cats worldwide are

wearing her clothes. The clothes keep sphynx cats warm, protect their skin from sunburn, and even soak up skin oils, so the cats need fewer baths.

Perfect Purr Facts

Melanie Manson's sphynx cats Smeagol and Zizzles have become cat supermodels. They appear in magazines, newspapers, and websites modeling their owner's creations.

Smeagol and Zizzles show off their sports tops.

Sphynx Movie Star

Mesa the sphynx cat is a feline movie star. She played the criminal mastermind Kitty Galore in the movie *Cats and Dogs 2: The Revenge of Kitty Galore*.

Kitty Galore is an evil, bald cat that plots to drive the world's dogs crazy using a terrible noise. Once humans are forced to get rid of their protective dog friends, Kitty Galore will take over the world!

Mesa appeared in some of the movie's scenes. In other scenes, **computer-generated images** (CGI) of Mesa were used. The movie's CGI artists filmed and studied Mesa's movements and behavior. Then they used their research to create the CGI character on computers.

Sphynx cats make smart, loving pets. Some are even fashion models and movie stars. Are these bald beauties the coolest cats around?

Mesa, the sphynx movie star

Perfect Purr Facts

Like all the animal characters in *Cats and Dogs* 2, Kitty Galore is able to talk. Her evil voice was provided by movie star Bette Midler.

Bette Midler

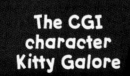

The CGI character Kitty Galore

29

Glossary

allergy (A-lur-jee) When a person's body reacts badly to something such as an animal or type of food. An allergy may make a person sneeze, get sore skin, vomit, or become seriously ill.

ancestors (AN-ses-terz) Relatives that lived long ago.

breed (BREED) A type of cat or other animal. Also, the word used to describe the act of mating two animals in order to produce young.

breeder (BREED-er) A person who breeds animals and sells them.

computer-generated images (kum-PYOO-ter-jeh-nuh-rayt-ed IH-mij-ez) Pictures made on a computer, such as moving, talking animals for movies.

down (DOWN) Short, soft hair, or fur, that can hardly be seen.

expression (ik-SPREH-shun) The look on a person or animal's face.

felines (FEE-lynz) Cats or other members of the cat family, such as a lion or a tiger.

groom (GROOM) To clean by licking, washing, or brushing.

litter (LIH-ter) A group of baby animals all born to the same mother at the same time.

littermates (LIH-ter maytz) Brother or sister animals born to the same mother at the same time.

mates (MAYTZ) To put male and female animals together so they produce young.

pads (PADZ) Soft cushions of flesh on the underside of an animal's foot.

saliva (suh-LY-vuh) The liquid in the mouth that starts to break down food and helps food slide down the throat.

unique (yoo-NEEK) The only one of its kind.

Websites

Due to the changing nature of Internet links, PowerKids Press has developed an online list of websites related to the subject of this book. This site is updated regularly. Please use this link to access the list:

www.powerkidslinks.com/cac/sphy/

Read More

Landau, Elaine. *Sphynx Are the Best!*. The Best Cats Ever. Minneapolis, MN: Lerner Publishing Group, 2011.

Mattern, Joanne. *Sphynx Cats*. All About Cats. Mankato, MN: Capstone Press, 2011.

Silverstein, Alvin, and Virginia Silverstein. *Hairless Cats: Cool Pets!*. Far-Out and Unusual Pets. Berkeley Heights, NJ: Enslow Publishers, 2011.

Index